KOH SAMUI, THAILAND

TRAVEL GUIDE 2024

A COMPREHENSIVE AND UPDATED GUIDEBOOK TO UNVEILING THE ATTRACTIONS AND HIDDEN GEMS OF KOH SAMUI FOR TRAVELERS

REX M. JASON

SCAN THE QR CODE BELOW TO GET ACCESS TO MORE BOOKS BY THE AUTHOR

TABLE OF CONTENT

CHAPTER 3: BEST PLACES TO EAT IN KOH SAMUI 66

CHAPTER 4: SHOPPING IN KOH SAMUI 83

INTRODUCTION

Once upon a time, there was a young couple called Jack and Emily who were searching for a romantic holiday. They chose to fly to Koh Samui, Thailand, expecting to discover a tranquil and lovely resort. As soon as they arrived, they were captivated by the island's natural splendor. The crystal-clear oceans, beautiful sandy beaches, and lush foliage were magnificent.

Jack and Emily spent their days exploring the island's various attractions, from the breathtaking waterfalls to the secret coves. They also tried their hand at scuba diving, a popular sport in Koh Samui. But what made their journey remarkable was the warmth and friendliness of the villagers they encountered along the route.

One day, Jack and Emily came to a little town where they encountered a group of youngsters who were living in poverty. Despite their challenging circumstances, the children greeted them with open arms and showed them their way of life. Jack and Emily were greatly impressed by their strength and resolve, and they realized they had to do something to assist.

They spent the remainder of their vacation helping at a local charity that assisted the children and their families. Through their job, they acquired a feeling of purpose and satisfaction that they had been lacking in their lives. When it came time to depart Koh Samui, Jack and Emily knew that they would always carry the memories of their journey and the lessons they learned with them.

Welcome to Koh Samui, Thailand, a tropical paradise that is guaranteed to fascinate and inspire you. With its magnificent beaches, rich foliage, and crystal-clear seas, Koh Samui is a resort that offers something for everyone. Whether you're searching for leisure, adventure, or an opportunity to give back to the community, Koh Samui offers it all. From the busy streets of the city to the calm serenity of the surrounding countryside, Koh Samui provides a unique combination of technology and heritage. You may tour historic temples, enjoy wonderful street cuisine, or just soak up the sun on one of the island's numerous beaches.

But what sets Koh Samui unique is the kindness and generosity of its people. Whether you're a seasoned traveler or a first-time guest, you'll be greeted with open arms and treated like family. And if you're searching for a chance to make a difference, Koh Samui provides various options to volunteer and give back to the community. So, come and explore the enchantment of Koh Samui for yourself. Whether you're here for a week or a month, you're sure to depart with memories that will last a lifetime.

CHAPTER 1: ABOUT KOH SAMUI

Koh Samui is a picturesque island situated in the Gulf of Thailand, noted for its breathtaking beaches, lush foliage, and bustling nightlife. It is the second-largest island in Thailand and is a famous tourist destination for people from all over the globe.

The island is home to a diverse variety of attractions, from historic temples and cultural relics to contemporary commercial complexes and luxury resorts.

One of the most famous sights on the island is the Big Buddha Temple, which has a 12-meter-tall golden Buddha statue that can be seen from kilometers away. Other significant temples include Wat Plai Laem and Wat

Khunaram, which are home to the mummified remains of a renowned monk.

Koh Samui is also recognized for its gorgeous beaches, which provide a variety of activities such as swimming, sunbathing, and water sports.

Some of the most popular beaches on the island are Chaweng Beach, Lamai Beach, and Bophut Beach. These beaches are surrounded by restaurants, cafes, and stores, making them the ideal destination to spend a day or evening.

For those searching for action, Koh Samui offers a choice of activities such as zip-lining,

ATV rides, and elephant trekking. The island is also home to numerous national parks, including Ang Thong National Marine Park, which is noted for its magnificent limestone cliffs, secret lagoons, and clean beaches.

Koh Samui is also recognized for its nightlife, with a choice of pubs, clubs, and restaurants that appeal to all tastes. The island is especially popular with backpackers and young visitors, who throng to the bars and clubs in Chaweng and Lamai.

In terms of lodging, Koh Samui provides a variety of alternatives to suit all budgets, from inexpensive hostels and guesthouses to luxury resorts and villas.

Many of the facilities on the island offer spa treatments, yoga courses, and other wellness activities, making it the ideal spot to rest and decompress.

Overall, Koh Samui is a gorgeous island that provides something for everyone. Whether you're searching for adventure, leisure, or busy nightlife, you're sure to find it on this lovely island in Thailand.

Why Visit Koh Samui

Koh Samui is a lovely island situated in the Gulf of Thailand, and it is one of the most famous tourist attractions in the country. There are numerous reasons why you should visit Koh Samui, and in this note, we will cover some of the top reasons why this island should be on your travel bucket list.

First and foremost, Koh Samui is recognized for its magnificent beaches. The island is home to some of the most stunning beaches in Thailand, with crystal-clear seas, silky white sand, and palm palms swinging in the air.

Whether you're wanting to relax and soak up the sun or enjoy water activities like snorkeling, diving, or kayaking, Koh Samui offers a beach that will meet your requirements. Some of the most popular beaches on the island are Chaweng Beach, Lamai Beach, and Bophut Beach.

In addition to its beaches, Koh Samui is also noted for its natural beauty. The island is home to numerous national parks, including Ang Thong National Marine Park, which is noted for its magnificent limestone cliffs, secret lagoons, and clean beaches. The park is a popular location for day visits and provides a variety of activities such as kayaking, hiking, and snorkeling.

Koh Samui is also an excellent location for individuals interested in culture and history. The island is home to various historic temples and cultural attractions, notably the Big Buddha Temple, which includes a 12-meter-tall golden Buddha statue that can be seen from kilometers away.

Other significant temples include Wat Plai Laem and Wat Khunaram, which are home to the mummified remains of a renowned monk.

For those searching for action, Koh Samui offers a choice of activities such as zip-lining, ATV rides, and elephant trekking. The island is also home to various water parks, including the Coco Splash Adventure & Water Park, which is a perfect spot to cool down on a hot day.

Koh Samui is also recognized for its nightlife, with a choice of pubs, clubs, and restaurants that appeal to all tastes. The island is especially popular with backpackers and young visitors, who throng to the bars and clubs in Chaweng and Lamai. In terms of lodging, Koh Samui provides a variety of alternatives to suit all budgets, from inexpensive hostels and guesthouses to luxury resorts and villas. Many of the facilities on the island offer spa treatments, yoga courses, and other wellness activities, making it the ideal spot to rest and decompress.

Overall, Koh Samui is a gorgeous island that provides something for everyone. Whether you're searching for adventure, leisure, or busy nightlife, you're sure to find it on this lovely island in Thailand. So, if you're planning a vacation to Thailand, make sure to include Koh Samui in your itinerary.

When to Visit Koh Samui

Koh Samui is a picturesque island situated in the Gulf of Thailand. It is a famous tourist destination noted for its magnificent beaches, crystal-clear seas, and lush tropical vegetation. The island has a tropical climate, which means that it is warm and humid throughout the year.

However, there are specific periods of the year when it is ideal to visit Koh Samui. The peak season on Koh Samui runs from December through February. During this period, the weather is dry and sunny, with temperatures ranging from 25°C to 30°C.

The sea is quiet, making it suitable for swimming and water sports. This is also the peak tourist season, so anticipate crowds and increased expenses for lodging and activities.

The shoulder season on Koh Samui spans from March through May. The weather is still warm and bright, although there may be intermittent rain showers. The water is still calm, and the people are beginning to clear away. This is a fantastic time to come if you want to escape the crowds and enjoy reduced costs.

The low season on Koh Samui spans from June through September. This is the rainy season, with occasional torrential downpours and thunderstorms. However, the rain generally doesn't linger long, and the sun comes out again. The sea may be turbulent at this time, so swimming and water sports may not be feasible. However, now is a fantastic time to come if you want to experience lesser costs and fewer people.

The monsoon season in Koh Samui spans from October through November. This is the wettest season of the year, with heavy rain and high winds. The sea may be choppy, and many water sports and activities may be canceled. This is not the best time to visit Koh Samui since many shops may be closed, and the weather may be unpredictable.

In conclusion, the ideal time to visit Koh Samui is from December to February, during the peak season. However, if you want to dodge the crowds and enjoy lesser pricing, the shoulder season from March to May is also a fantastic time to come.

If you don't mind periodic rain showers and want to enjoy lower pricing, the low season from June to September is a wonderful alternative.

However, it is advisable to avoid the monsoon season from October to November, since the weather may be unpredictable and many establishments may be closed.

Getting Around Koh Samui

Getting to Koh Samui is quite straightforward, with various transportation choices available.

Taxis are a prominent means of transportation on the island. They are widely accessible at the airport, ferry ports, and main tourist locations. Taxis in Koh Samui do not have meters; therefore, it is advised to negotiate the rate before beginning the ride to prevent any misunderstandings.

Taxis are somewhat pricey compared to other kinds of transportation, but they are convenient and pleasant.

Motorbikes and scooters are also common methods of transportation in Koh Samui. They are available for hire at numerous sites across the island. Renting a motorcycle or scooter is a terrific way to explore the island at your leisure.

However, it is crucial to wear a helmet and drive safely, since the roads in Koh Samui may be small and twisty.

For those who prefer an eco-friendlier means of transportation, bicycles are available for hire at many sites across the island. Bicycles are a terrific way to explore the island at a leisurely pace, and they are also a good way to keep active and healthy.

Finally, private automobile hiring is also accessible on the island. This is an excellent alternative for individuals who wish to tour the island at their leisure and enjoy the comfort of a private car. Private car hire may be booked via hotels or travel companies, and fees vary based on the kind of vehicle and the period of the rental.

In conclusion, traveling to Koh Samui is quite straightforward, with various transportation alternatives accessible. Taxis, songthaews, motorcycles, scooters, bicycles, and private automobile rentals are all accessible on the island. It is crucial to pick the form of transportation that best meets your demands and budget.

Whatever form of transportation you pick, be sure to tour the island and enjoy everything that Koh Samui has to offer.

Visa Requirements

Koh Samui is a renowned tourist destination situated in Thailand, and as such, it is crucial to understand the visa requirements for visiting the island. The visa requirements for Koh Samui vary depending on the nationality of the traveler and the duration of their stay.

For tourists from many countries, a visa is not needed for stays of up to 30 days. This includes tourists from the United States, Canada, the United Kingdom, Australia, and many more nations.

Visitors from these countries may visit Thailand without a visa and remain for up to 30 days. For travelers who desire to remain longer than 30 days, a visa is necessary.

There are numerous sorts of visas available, including tourist visas, business visas, and education visas.

Tourist visas are the most prevalent form of visa for tourists to Koh Samui, and they enable travelers to remain in Thailand for up to 60 days. To get a tourist visa for Thailand, travelers must apply at a Thai embassy or consulate in their home country. The application procedure normally involves a passport, a completed visa application form, and a fee. Visitors may also be required to produce extra papers, such as evidence of onward travel or proof of financial assistance.

For those who desire to remain in Thailand for more than 60 days, a long-stay visa may be necessary. Long-stay visas are available for travelers who intend to remain in Thailand for up to one year. These visas are often provided for objectives such as retirement, business, or education.

To get a long-stay visa for Thailand, tourists must apply at a Thai embassy or consulate in their home country. The application procedure normally involves a passport, a completed visa application form, and a cost.

Visitors may also be needed to produce extra papers, such as evidence of retirement or proof of attendance in an educational program. It is essential to remember that visa requirements might change at any moment, and travelers should check with the Thai embassy or consulate in their home country for the most up-to-date information.

Visitors should also check that their passport is valid for at least six months beyond their anticipated stay in Thailand.

In conclusion, the visa requirements for Koh Samui vary on the country of the traveler and the duration of their stay. Tourist from many countries may enter Thailand without a visa for stays of up to 30 days, but tourists who intend to stay longer than 30 days may need a visa. It is necessary to check with the Thai embassy or consulate in your home country for the most up-to-date information on visa requirements.

CHAPTER 2: TOP ATTRACTIONS IN KOH SAMUI

Koh Samui is a gorgeous island situated in Thailand, noted for its breathtaking beaches, rich foliage, and active culture. There are several outstanding attractions on Koh Samui that tourists should not miss.

One of the most famous sights is the Big Buddha Temple, which has a 12-meter-tall golden Buddha statue and spectacular views over the island. Another must-visit site is the Na Muang Cascade, which is a stunning natural cascade surrounded by thick flora.

For those interested in cultural experiences, the Fisherman's Village in Bophut is a terrific spot to visit. It boasts traditional Thai architecture, small markets, and great seafood eateries. The Wat Plai Laem temple is also a major cultural site, with elaborate Buddhist figures and gorgeous architecture.

Koh Samui is also recognized for its gorgeous beaches, such as Chaweng Beach and Lamai Beach, which provide crystal blue seas and white sand. Visitors may also take a boat cruise to see the adjacent islands, such as Koh Tao and Koh Phangan.

Overall, Koh Samui provides a broad choice of things for tourists to enjoy, from cultural experiences to natural marvels and stunning beaches.

Chaweng Beach

Chaweng Beach is one of the most popular and picturesque beaches in Koh Samui, Thailand. It is situated on the east coast of the island and spans 7 kilometers, making it the longest beach on the island.

The beach is famed for its crystal blue seas, silky white sand, and breathtaking views of the Gulf of Thailand.

Chaweng Beach is a terrific spot to relax and soak up the sun. The beach is bordered by palm trees, offering plenty of shade for those who wish to escape the sun. There are also several coastal restaurants and pubs where guests can have a cool drink or a wonderful meal while taking in the stunning views.

For those who prefer to be more active, Chaweng Beach provides a selection of water sports activities, such as jet skiing, parasailing, and kayaking. Visitors may also take a boat cruise to visit the local islands or go snorkeling to witness the beautiful aquatic life.

In the evening, Chaweng Beach comes alive with a busy entertainment scene. There are several pubs and nightclubs where guests may dance the night away or enjoy live music performances.

The beach also offers frequent fire performances, which are a must-see for anyone visiting Koh Samui.

Chaweng Beach is also conveniently positioned near many other attractions on the island.

Visitors may easily visit the surrounding Fisherman's Village in Bophut or the Big Buddha Temple, which are both only a short drive away.

Overall, Chaweng Beach is a lovely and vibrant place that provides something for everyone.

Whether you want to relax on the beach, enjoy water sports activities, or experience the active nightlife, Chaweng Beach is a must-visit site in Koh Samui, Thailand.

Big Buddha Temple

The Big Buddha Temple, commonly known as Wat Phra Yai, is one of the most distinctive and popular sights in Koh Samui, Thailand.

Located on a tiny island off the northeast coast of the island, the temple is home to a large golden Buddha statue that stands 12 meters tall and can be seen from miles away. The temple was established in 1972 and has since become a prominent religious and cultural landmark for both residents and visitors.

Visitors may visit the temple through a causeway that links the island to the mainland. As you approach the temple, you will be met with the spectacular sight of the big Buddha statue, which is encircled by smaller sculptures of various Buddhist deities.

The temple grounds are nicely maintained and give wonderful views of the surrounding region. Visitors may visit the numerous structures and shrines on the grounds, including the main prayer hall, which includes a giant sitting Buddha statue and beautiful paintings representing incidents from Buddhist mythology.

One of the most unusual aspects of the Big Buddha Temple is the collection of little bells that hang from the eaves of the structures. Visitors are invited to ring the bells as they go around the temple grounds, which is thought to bring good luck and blessings.

The temple is also home to a multitude of stores and kiosks offering souvenirs, religious products, and local handicrafts. Visitors may also have a meal or a refreshing drink at one of the numerous restaurants and cafés situated on the island.

The Big Buddha Temple is a must-visit attraction for anyone visiting Koh Samui. It gives a unique and intriguing look into Thai culture and religion, as well as spectacular vistas and picture possibilities. Whether you are a history enthusiast, a spiritual seeker, or just searching for a lovely and serene spot to visit, the Big Buddha Temple is guaranteed to make a lasting impression.

Fisherman's Village

The Fisherman's Village in Koh Samui, Thailand, is a lovely location that provides tourists with a look into the island's rich cultural past. Located on the northern shore of the island, the town is a renowned tourist attraction that draws people from all over the globe.

The hamlet was originally a flourishing fishing community, and many of the ancient buildings and structures have been maintained and rebuilt, giving the region a distinctive and genuine character.

Visitors may meander through the tiny alleys and passageways, seeing the historic wooden buildings and stores that line the path.

One of the great attractions of the Fisherman's Village is the weekly night market, which takes place every Friday evening. The market is a lively and colorful event, with sellers selling everything from local handicrafts and souvenirs to wonderful street food and fresh seafood.

In addition to the night market, the Fisherman's Village is home to a variety of superb restaurants and cafés, dishing up a mix of local and foreign food. Visitors may have a meal or a drink while taking in the wonderful views of the ocean and the surrounding hills.

The hamlet is also home to a variety of art galleries and shops, displaying the work of local artists and designers. Visitors may peruse the stores and galleries, picking up unique and handcrafted goods to take home with them.

For those interested in history and culture, the Fisherman's Village is home to a variety of noteworthy sites and attractions. The Wat Plai Laem temple, situated only a short distance from the town, is a wonderful example of traditional Thai architecture and boasts a big statue of the goddess Guanyin.

Overall, the Fisherman's Village in Koh Samui is a must-visit place for anybody traveling to the island. With its rich cultural past, breathtaking surroundings, and active environment, it gives tourists a unique and remarkable experience that is guaranteed to make a lasting impression.

Hin Ta and Hin Yai Rocks

The Hin Ta and Hin Yai Rocks, popularly known as the Grandfather and Grandmother Rocks, are one of the most prominent tourist sites on the island of Koh Samui, Thailand. These unusual rock formations are situated on the southern shore of the island, near the town of Lamai, and are a must-visit location for anybody coming to the region.

The rocks are called from their similarity to male and female genitalia, with the Hin Ta rock resembling a male organ and the Hin Yai rock resembling a female organ. The rocks are formed of granite and have been carved over thousands of years by the natural forces of wind and water.

According to local tradition, the rocks were built by a couple who were stranded on the island and died there.

The boulders are claimed to represent a sign of their love and commitment to one other and are regarded to be a holy location by the local people.

Visitors to the Hin Ta and Hin Yai Rocks may explore the region and take in the spectacular views of the ocean and surrounding environment.

There are also a lot of merchants offering souvenirs and food, making it a nice spot to stop and take a break from touring the island.

In addition to the rocks themselves, the region surrounding the Hin Ta and Hin Yai Rocks is home to a variety of additional attractions and activities. Visitors may take a boat tour of the adjacent islands, go snorkeling or scuba diving in the crystal-clear seas, or just relax on the gorgeous beaches.

Overall, the Hin Ta and Hin Yai Rocks are a unique and intriguing location that provides tourists with a look into the natural beauty and cultural legacy of Koh Samui.

Whether you are interested in history, culture, or just enjoying the gorgeous environment, this is a must-visit site that is guaranteed to make a lasting impact.

Na Muang Waterfalls

Na Muang Waterfalls are one of the most renowned tourist attractions on the island of Koh Samui, Thailand. Located in the middle of the island, these gorgeous waterfalls are a must-visit site for anybody visiting the region.

The name Na Muang means "purple waterfalls" in Thai, and the waterfalls acquire their name from the purple tint of the rocks that surround them. The waterfalls are two different falls, with Na Muang 1 being the biggest of the two and Na Muang 2 being somewhat smaller.

Na Muang 1 is the most popular of the two waterfalls and is readily accessible by vehicle or motorcycle. Visitors may park at the foot of the falls and take a short climb up to the top, where they can enjoy beautiful views of the surrounding forest and the cascade itself.

The falls are around 30 meters high and drop down into a huge pool at the foot, making it a popular site for swimming and cooling down on a hot day.

Na Muang 2 is situated a short distance from Na Muang 1 and is significantly more difficult to access. Visitors must travel through the forest for around 30 minutes to reach the falls, but the effort is well worth it.

Na Muang 2 is smaller than Na Muang 1 but is still a magnificent site to see. The falls drop down into several pools, making it a popular area for swimming and relaxation.

In addition to the waterfalls itself, the region surrounding Na Muang is home to a variety of additional attractions and activities.

Visitors may explore the adjacent rainforest on foot or by ATV, go zip-lining over the trees, or just relax on the gorgeous beaches that are available nearby.

Overall, Na Muang Waterfalls is a must-visit location for anybody visiting Koh Samui. Whether you are interested in nature, adventure, or just enjoying the gorgeous surroundings, this is a place that is guaranteed to make a lasting impression.

Secret Buddha Garden

The Secret Buddha Garden, also known as the Magic Garden or Heaven's Garden, is a hidden jewel found in the hills of Koh Samui, Thailand. This mysterious garden is a must-visit place for anybody visiting the island, as it provides a unique and captivating experience that is unlike anything else on the island.

The Secret Buddha Garden was established by a local farmer called Nim Thongsuk, who started developing the garden in 1976 at the age of 77.

Nim was motivated by a dream he had, in which he saw a group of angels who ordered him to establish a garden in the hills. He spent the next 25 years of his life constructing this wonderful garden, which is today a famous tourist destination on the island.

The garden is nestled in the hills of Koh Samui, and can only be accessed by a steep and twisting road that climbs up to the top of the hill. Once you arrive at the garden, you will be met with a breathtaking collection of sculptures, statues, and other pieces of art that are spread around the area.

The sculptures in the garden are fashioned from a range of materials, including stone, concrete, and wood. They show a broad variety of topics, including animals, people, and legendary beings. Each sculpture is unique and has its tale to tell, making the garden a fascinating location to explore.

One of the most stunning sculptures in the garden is the enormous Buddha statue that rests at the top of the hill. This statue is nearly 12 meters tall and is encircled by smaller sculptures of Buddha and other deities. The view from the summit of the hill is stunning and gives a panoramic view of the surrounding hills and shoreline.

In addition to the sculptures, the garden is also home to a variety of flora and trees, including exotic flowers, fruit trees, and bamboo. The garden is a beautiful and tranquil spot and is a fantastic place to rest and unwind after a long day of visiting the island.

Overall, the Secret Buddha Garden is a must-visit place for everyone visiting Koh Samui. It provides a unique and magical experience that is unlike anything else on the island and is a terrific spot to explore and appreciate the beauty of Thai culture and art.

Wat Plai Laem Temple

The Wat Plai Laem Temple is one of the most beautiful and distinctive temples in Koh Samui, Thailand. Located on the northeastern edge of the island, this temple is a must-visit location for anybody visiting Koh Samui.

The temple is recognized for its spectacular architecture, exquisite artwork, and attractive sculptures.

The temple was established in 2004 and is dedicated to the goddess of compassion and mercy, Guanyin. The temple is a combination of Thai and Chinese styles and has a big figure of Guanyin in the middle of the temple. The statue is nearly 18 meters tsall and is encircled by lesser sculptures of various deities.

One of the most outstanding elements of the temple is the enormous pond that surrounds the figure of Guanyin. The pond is packed with fish and turtles, and visitors may buy food to feed them. The pond is also home to a huge number of lotus blossoms, which contribute to the beauty of the temple.

The temple also contains a vast prayer hall, which is filled with beautiful artwork and paintings. The hall is a pleasant and tranquil spot, and guests are free to sit and contemplate or give prayers.

Another remarkable aspect of the temple is the enormous statue of the smiling Buddha, which is positioned near the entrance to the temple. The monument is almost 30 meters tall and is a popular site for shooting pictures. In addition to the main temple, there are also other minor temples and shrines situated on the grounds of the Wat Plai Laem Temple. These temples are devoted to numerous deities and provide visitors with a chance to learn more about Thai culture and religion.

Overall, the Wat Plai Laem Temple is a must-visit place for anybody visiting Koh Samui. The temple is a lovely and serene area and allows tourists an opportunity to enjoy the splendor of Thai culture and religion.

Samui Elephant Sanctuary

The Samui Elephant Sanctuary is a must-visit attraction for everyone visiting Koh Samui, Thailand. This sanctuary is committed to providing a secure and ethical home for elephants who have been rescued from the tourist and forestry industries. The refuge is nestled in the beautiful rainforest of Koh Samui and allows visitors an opportunity to contact these gorgeous creatures responsibly and sustainably.

The Samui Elephant Sanctuary was created in 2018 and is the first elephant sanctuary in Koh Samui. The sanctuary is home to six elephants, all of whom have been rescued from the tourist and logging sectors.

These elephants have gone through a lot of trauma and cruelty, and the sanctuary offers them a secure and serene environment where they may live out the remainder of their lives in peace.

One of the unusual qualities of the Samui Elephant Sanctuary is that visitors are not permitted to ride the elephants. This is because riding elephants may give them a lot of agony and anguish, and can also be harmful for both the elephants and the riders. Instead, visitors are encouraged to engage with the elephants in a more natural manner, such as feeding them, washing them, and strolling with them through the forest.

The sanctuary provides numerous different tour choices, ranging from a half-day trip to a full-day tour. During the trip, guests will get the chance to learn about the history and behavior of elephants, as well as the issues they face in Thailand.

Visitors will also get the option to feed the elephants, bathe them in the river, and stroll with them in the bush.

The Samui Elephant Sanctuary is devoted to sustainability and ethical tourism. The sanctuary employs solar power to produce energy, and all of the food supplied to the elephants is locally sourced and organic. The refuge also employs local employees, and a percentage of the earnings from the trips goes towards assisting local communities and conservation initiatives.

Overall, the Samui Elephant Sanctuary is a must-visit location for everyone visiting Koh Samui. The sanctuary provides visitors an opportunity to engage with elephants responsibly and sustainably, while also learning about the issues affecting these beautiful creatures in Thailand. Whether you are an animal lover or just interested in sustainable tourism, the Samui Elephant Sanctuary is a place that should not be missed.

CHAPTER 3: BEST PLACES TO EAT IN KOH SAMUI

Koh Samui, Thailand, is a food lover's delight, with a broad selection of restaurants and street food sellers serving excellent and genuine Thai cuisine. From fresh seafood to spicy curries, there is something for everyone on Koh Samui. Here are some of the greatest places to dine in Koh Samui:

1. The Jungle Club: This restaurant is set on a mountaintop above Chaweng Beach and provides beautiful views of the island. The menu contains a combination of Thai and foreign cuisine, featuring dishes like pad Thai, green curry, and grilled fish.

The Jungle Club is also noted for its cocktails, which are created with fresh fruit and herbs.

2. Fisherman's Town: This lovely town on the north shore of Koh Samui is home to a variety of eateries and street food sellers. The seafood here is exceptionally fresh and excellent, with meals including grilled prawns, steaming fish, and seafood curry. The hamlet also includes a night market on Fridays, where you can try a variety of street cuisine.

3. Lamai Beach Night Market: This night market is situated in the village of Lamai, and is a terrific spot to enjoy local street cuisine.

The market is open every night and offers merchants selling anything from grilled meats to fresh fruit smoothies. Be sure to sample the pad Thai and mango sticky rice.

4. The Larder: This restaurant near Chaweng Beach is noted for its sophisticated Thai cuisine, featuring dishes like green curry risotto and tom yum soup with prawns. The restaurant also boasts a superb assortment of beverages and specialty brews.

5. H Bistro: This French restaurant in Fisherman's Village puts a unique touch on Thai cuisine, with dishes like duck confit with red curry sauce and green papaya salad with foie gras. The restaurant also offers an excellent wine list.

6. Khaw Glong Thai Restaurant: This restaurant near Chaweng Beach is recognized for its genuine Thai food, including dishes like massaman curry and stir-fried morning glory. The restaurant also boasts a wonderful assortment of vegetarian alternatives.

7. The Cliff Bar and Grill: This restaurant is built on a cliff overlooking the ocean and provides beautiful views of the sunset. The menu contains a combination of Thai and foreign cuisine, featuring delicacies like grilled shellfish and beef tenderloin. The restaurant also boasts a wonderful assortment of beverages and live music on weekends. Koh Samui is a food lover's paradise, with a broad selection of restaurants and street food sellers serving wonderful and genuine Thai cuisine. Whether you are seeking fresh seafood, spicy curries, or new takes on classic meals, there is something for everyone in Koh Samui.

Street Food

One of the most interesting features of Koh Samui's culture is its street food scene, which provides a broad range of excellent and genuine Thai cuisine. The street cuisine on Koh Samui reflects the island's many cultural influences, with tastes and ingredients from throughout Thailand and Southeast Asia.

From fiery curries to sweet pastries, there is something for everyone in Koh Samui's street food culture.

One of the most famous street food meals on Koh Samui is pad Thai, a stir-fried noodle dish prepared with shrimp, tofu, bean sprouts, and peanuts. This dish is a mainstay of Thai cuisine and can be found at practically every street food seller on the island. Another famous meal is som tam, a spicy green papaya salad that is a favorite among residents and visitors alike.

Seafood is also a prominent element of Koh Samui's street food scene, with sellers serving fresh grilled fish, prawns, and squid.

These meals are generally served with spicy dipping sauces and are a must-try for seafood enthusiasts. For those with a sweet craving, Koh Samui's street food scene provides a range of delicacies, including mango sticky rice, coconut ice cream, and banana pancakes. These delicious delights are excellent for a mid-day snack or a post-dinner splurge.

One of the best venues to enjoy Koh Samui's street food culture is the night markets, which are hosted in various locations throughout the island on different evenings of the week. These markets feature a broad selection of street food sellers, as well as local crafts and souvenirs.

One of the most popular night markets on Koh Samui is the Lamai Beach Night Market, which is open every night and has merchants selling anything from grilled meats to fresh fruit smoothies. Another famous market is the Fisherman's Village Night Market, which is held on Fridays and contains a variety of street food vendors and live music.

Overall, Koh Samui's street food culture is a must-try for everyone visiting the island. With its different tastes and ingredients, there is something for everyone to appreciate.

Whether you're searching for a quick snack or a full dinner, Koh Samui's street food sellers have got you covered.

Seafood

One of the most interesting features of Koh Samui's culture is its seafood scene, which provides a broad selection of tasty and genuine Thai seafood.

Seafood is a prominent element of Koh Samui's cuisine, with vendors offering fresh grilled fish, prawns, and squid.

These meals are generally served with spicy dipping sauces and are a must-try for seafood enthusiasts. The seafood on Koh Samui reflects the island's many cultural influences, with tastes and ingredients from throughout Thailand and Southeast Asia.

One of the most popular seafood meals on Koh Samui is grilled fish, which is generally served with a spicy dipping sauce prepared with chile, lime, and garlic. The fish is frequently marinated in a blend of herbs and spices before being grilled over an open flame, giving it a smokey and savory taste.

Another famous seafood meal on Koh Samui is prawn curry, which is prepared with fresh prawns cooked in a spicy coconut milk-based curry sauce. The curry is generally served with steamed rice and is popular among residents and visitors alike.

Squid is also a popular seafood on Koh Samui, with merchants serving grilled squid skewers and spicy squid salad. The grilled squid skewers are marinated in a blend of herbs and spices before being cooked over an open flame, giving them a smokey and savory flavor. The spicy squid salad is composed of fresh squid, chile, lime, and herbs, giving it a pleasant and spicy flavor.

For those searching for a more adventurous seafood experience, Koh Samui also offers a range of unique seafood delicacies, such as sea urchins, jellyfish, and sea snails.

These meals are not for the faint of heart, but for those eager to try something new, they provide a unique and remarkable gastronomic experience.

One of the best venues to enjoy Koh Samui's seafood scene is the local seafood markets, which are hosted in various locations across the island.

These markets provide a large range of fresh seafood, as well as local crafts and souvenirs.

Overall, Koh Samui's seafood scene is a must-try for everyone visiting the island. With its different tastes and ingredients, there is something for everyone to appreciate.

Whether you're searching for a quick snack or a complete seafood feast, Koh Samui's seafood sellers have got you covered.

Vegetarian and Vegan Options

One of the most interesting features of Koh Samui's culture is its culinary scene, which provides a broad range of tasty and genuine Thai cuisine. For individuals who follow a vegetarian or vegan diet, Koh Samui offers lots of alternatives to select from.

Thai food is noted for its use of fresh herbs and spices, making it a perfect alternative for vegetarians and vegans. Many Thai meals are inherently vegetarian or may be readily adjusted to be vegan.

One of the most popular vegetarian meals in Thailand is Pad Thai, which is prepared with rice noodles, tofu, veggies, and peanuts. Other popular vegetarian recipes include Tom Yum soup, vegetable stir-fry, and green curry. For those who follow a vegan diet, Koh Samui offers lots of possibilities as well.

Many Thai meals may be turned vegan by simply eliminating the meat or shellfish and using vegetable stock instead of chicken or beef broth. Vegan alternatives include vegetable curries, stir-fries, and noodle meals.

In addition to traditional Thai food, Koh Samui now offers a growing number of vegetarian and vegan eateries. One of the most popular is Green Light Cafe, which provides a range of vegan and vegetarian cuisine, including smoothie bowls, salads, and vegan burgers.

Another popular alternative is Karma Sutra, which serves a range of vegetarian and vegan cuisine, including Indian curries and vegan sushi.

For those searching for a more upmarket eating experience, Koh Samui also boasts some high-end vegetarian and vegan eateries.

One of the most popular is Pure Vegan Heaven, which provides a range of vegan cuisine produced using organic and locally sourced ingredients.

Another popular alternative is Anantara Bophut Koh Samui Resort, which provides a vegan-tasting menu comprising foods such as vegan sushi and veggie curry.

In addition to eateries, Koh Samui also boasts various health food shops and marketplaces that provide a range of vegetarian and vegan items. One of the most popular is Samui Health Shop, which sells a range of organic and vegan items, including fresh vegetables, snacks, and vitamins.

Overall, Koh Samui's vegetarian and vegan alternatives are extensive and diversified. Whether you're seeking traditional Thai food or upmarket vegan dining, Koh Samui offers something for everyone. With its fresh ingredients and vivid tastes, Koh Samui's vegetarian and vegan food is a must-try for anybody visiting the island.

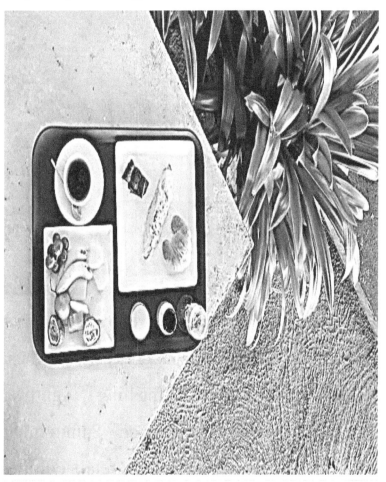

CHAPTER 4: SHOPPING IN KOH SAMUI

Koh Samui, Thailand, is a renowned tourist destination noted for its magnificent beaches, colorful culture, and thrilling nightlife. However, one part of Koh Samui that sometimes gets ignored is its retail culture.

From lively markets to high-end shops, Koh Samui provides a broad array of shopping alternatives for tourists to enjoy.

One of the most popular shopping venues in Koh Samui is the night market. These markets are hosted at various sites across the island on different evenings of the week and provide a broad range of things, including apparel, accessories, souvenirs, and street food.

The most prominent night markets are the Fisherman's Village Night Market, which is held every Friday, and the Chaweng Night Market, which is held every night.

Another famous shopping attraction in Koh Samui is the Central Festival Samui retail mall. This is situated in the middle of Chaweng and provides a broad selection of high-end antiques, foreign brands, and local merchants.

Visitors may get anything from luxury apparel and accessories to electronics and household items. For those searching for unique and handcrafted things, Koh Samui features various artisan markets and boutiques.

One of the most popular is the Bophut Fisherman's Village Walking Street, which is held every Friday and provides a range of handcrafted goods, apparel, and souvenirs. Another popular choice is the Lamai Sunday Night Market, which provides a range of handcrafted products, including jewelry, apparel, and home décor.

In addition to marketplaces and malls, Koh Samui also boasts various specialty businesses that cater to unique interests. For example, the Samui Elephant Sanctuary Gift Shop sells a range of elephant-themed products, including clothes, accessories, and home décor.

The Samui Art Gallery features a range of local artwork, including paintings, sculptures, and photography.

For those searching for luxury shopping experiences, Koh Samui features various high-end shops and designer outlets.

One of the most popular is the Nikki Beach Lifestyle Boutique, which provides a selection of luxury apparel, accessories, and home items.

Another popular alternative is the Samui Luxury Collection, which provides a selection of high-end brands, including Gucci, Prada, and Louis Vuitton.

Overall, Koh Samui's retail culture provides something for everyone, from vibrant night markets to high-end shops.

Whether you're seeking unusual souvenirs, homemade crafts, or luxury products, Koh Samui offers lots of possibilities to discover.

With its lively culture and diversified retail environment, Koh Samui is a must-visit destination for every shopaholic.

Shopping Malls

One part of Koh Samui that sometimes gets ignored is its retail culture. From lively markets to high-end shops, Koh Samui provides a broad array of shopping alternatives for tourists to enjoy.

One of the most popular shopping venues in Koh Samui is the retail mall.

The Central Festival Samui shopping mall is situated in the middle of Chaweng and provides a broad choice of high-end boutiques, worldwide brands, and local retailers.

Visitors may get anything from luxury apparel and accessories to electronics and household items. The mall is located across three stories and contains a range of stores, restaurants, and entertainment opportunities. The mall is air-conditioned, making it a fantastic spot to escape the heat and humidity of Koh Samui.

Another major shopping mall in Koh Samui is the Tesco Lotus Mall. This mall is situated in the northern portion of the island and is a fantastic area to buy groceries, home products, and electronics. The mall contains a huge Tesco Lotus supermarket, as well as a range of other stores and eateries. The mall is air-conditioned and has adequate parking, making it a pleasant location to shop.

For those searching for luxury shopping experiences, Koh Samui features various high-end shops and designer outlets.

One of the most popular is the Nikki Beach Lifestyle Boutique, which provides a selection of luxury apparel, accessories, and home items. Another popular alternative is the Samui Luxury Collection, which provides a selection of high-end brands, including Gucci, Prada, and Louis Vuitton.

In addition to the bigger commercial malls, Koh Samui also boasts various smaller shopping complexes and plazas. The Wharf Samui is a famous retail and eating location situated in Bophut. The plaza contains a variety of stores, restaurants, and bars, as well as a weekly night market. The plaza is meant to imitate a small fishing hamlet and has a distinct feel.

Overall, Koh Samui's retail environment provides something for everyone, from vibrant night markets to high-end shops and shopping centers.

Whether you're seeking unusual souvenirs, homemade crafts, or luxury products, Koh Samui offers lots of possibilities to discover. With its lively culture and diversified retail environment, Koh Samui is a must-visit destination for every shopaholic.

Souvenirs and Handicrafts

Visitors to Koh Samui may discover a broad selection of unique and exquisite handicrafts and souvenirs that represent the island's rich cultural past.

One of the most popular handicrafts on Koh Samui is coconut shell cutting. The island is noted for its plentiful coconut palms, and native craftsmen have developed a distinctive way of carving elaborate motifs into the shells. Visitors may discover a variety of coconut shell carvings, including bowls, cups, and ornamental objects. These carvings make for attractive and distinctive mementos that are guaranteed to wow.

Another prominent specialty in Koh Samui is silk weaving. Local weavers employ ancient methods to make gorgeous silk textiles in a range of colors and designs.

Visitors may discover a range of silk goods, including scarves, shawls, and clothes. These goods make for sumptuous and beautiful keepsakes that are likely to be loved for years to come.

Koh Samui is also recognized for its distinctive jewelry. Local artists employ a range of materials, including silver, gold, and precious stones, to produce gorgeous and detailed pieces.

Visitors may discover a range of jewelry, including necklaces, bracelets, and earrings. These sculptures make magnificent and distinctive mementos that are guaranteed to be loved.

For those searching for more traditional souvenirs, Koh Samui provides a range of possibilities. Visitors may discover a variety of handcrafted products, including ceramics, wood sculptures, and woven baskets.

These objects are generally manufactured using traditional processes and represent the island's rich cultural past. Visitors may also discover a range of traditional apparel, including sarongs and batik textiles.

One of the finest locations to discover handicrafts and souvenirs in Koh Samui is at the island's various markets. The night markets, in particular, are a terrific location to discover unusual and handcrafted things.

Visitors may visit a variety of kiosks offering anything from handcrafted jewelry to traditional attire. The markets also provide a variety of street food and entertainment, making for a pleasant and energetic scene.

CHAPTER 5: NIGHTLIFE IN KOH SAMUI

Koh Samui, Thailand, is a renowned tourist destination noted for its magnificent beaches, colorful culture, and thrilling nightlife. The island provides a broad array of entertainment alternatives for guests, from beach parties to nightclubs to cultural events.

Whether you're searching for a crazy night out or a calmer evening, Koh Samui offers something for everyone.

One of the most famous nightlife spots in Koh Samui is Chaweng Beach. This region is noted for its vibrant atmosphere and number of pubs and nightclubs. Visitors may enjoy a range of music venues, from live bands to DJs playing the newest songs. The beach itself is also a popular area for parties, with fire performances and other entertainment regularly taking place.

Another famous nightlife spot on Koh Samui is Lamai Beach. This region is noted for its more laid-back attitude, with a variety of pubs and eateries giving it a more casual feel. Visitors may enjoy live music and entertainment, as well as a choice of food and drink options.

For those searching for a more cultural experience, Koh Samui also offers a selection of traditional acts and performances. The Thai Boxing Stadium in Chaweng is a renowned site for Muay Thai bouts, while the Samui Cultural Center provides traditional dance and music events.

In addition to the conventional nightlife alternatives, Koh Samui also provides a selection of unique experiences.

Visitors may take a sunset boat around the island, enjoying beverages and music while taking in the spectacular sights. The island also provides a variety of beach parties, with events typically taking place at renowned sites like Ark Bar and Nikki Beach.

Overall, Koh Samui's nightlife culture provides something for everyone. Whether you're looking for a crazy night out or a more peaceful evening, the island provides lots of possibilities to explore.

With its lively culture and eclectic entertainment scene, Koh Samui is a must-visit location for anybody interested in experiencing the finest of Thailand's nightlife.

Night Bars and Pubs

One of the most popular nightlife locations in Koh Samui is its nightclubs and pubs. Chaweng Beach is the most popular place for nightlife in Koh Samui, and it is home to a variety of nightclubs and pubs. Visitors may enjoy a range of music venues, from live bands to DJs playing the newest songs. The beach itself is also a popular area for parties, with fire performances and other entertainment regularly taking place.

Some of the most popular nightclubs and pubs in Chaweng Beach are Green Mango, Reggae Pub, and Sound Club.

Lamai Beach is another famous spot for nightlife in Koh Samui, and it provides a more laid-back ambiance than Chaweng Beach. Visitors may enjoy live music and entertainment, as well as a choice of food and drink options.

Some of the most popular nightclubs and pubs in Lamai Beach are Shamrock Irish Pub, Fusion Club, and Bauhaus Bar.

For those searching for a more upmarket experience, Koh Samui also offers a range of high-end nightclubs and pubs.

The WOO Bar at the W Beach Club of Koh Samui is a popular place for people seeking a lavish night out with its spectacular ocean views and sophisticated environment.

The Beach Club of the InterContinental Samui Baan Taling Ngam Resort is another popular spot, with its trendy décor and beachfront position.

In addition to conventional nightclubs and pubs, Koh Samui also provides a range of unique experiences.

Visitors may take a sunset boat around the island, enjoying beverages and music while taking in the spectacular sights. The island also provides a variety of beach parties, with events typically taking place at renowned sites like Ark Bar and Nikki Beach.

Overall, Koh Samui's nightclubs and pubs provide something for everyone. Whether you're looking for a crazy night out or a more peaceful evening, the island provides lots of possibilities to explore. With its lively culture and eclectic entertainment scene, Koh Samui is a must-visit location for anybody interested in experiencing the finest of Thailand's nightlife.

Beach Clubs

One of the most popular attractions on the island is the beach club scene. These clubs provide a unique experience for guests, mixing the beauty of the beach with the thrill of a party scene. In this exhaustive note, we will investigate the beach clubs of Koh Samui, Thailand.

1. Nikki Beach Club: Nikki Beach Club is one of the most renowned beach clubs in Koh Samui. It is situated on Lipa Noi Beach and provides a wonderful experience for guests.

The club offers a huge swimming pool, luxurious sun loungers, and a café providing wonderful cuisine and beverages. Nikki Beach Club is noted for its wild events, with DJs playing music till the early hours of the morning.

2. Beach Republic: Beach Republic is another famous beach club in Koh Samui. It is situated on Lamai Beach and provides a more easygoing environment than some of the other clubs on the island. The club offers a huge swimming pool, luxurious sun loungers, and a café providing wonderful cuisine and beverages. Beach Republic is famed for its Sunday brunch, which is a must-try for guests.

3. W Beach Club: W Beach Club is situated on Mae Nam Beach and provides a unique experience for tourists. The club offers a huge swimming pool, luxurious sun loungers, and a café providing wonderful cuisine and beverages. W Beach Club is recognized for its breathtaking views of the ocean and its relaxing attitude.

4. Coco Tam's: Coco Tam's is situated on Bophut Beach and provides a more laid-back environment than some of the other clubs on the island. The club has comfy bean bags, a café with wonderful cuisine and beverages, and a fire display in the evenings. Coco Tam's is recognized for its breathtaking views of the ocean and its calm ambiance.

5. Ark Bar Beach Club: Ark Bar Beach Club is situated on Chaweng Beach and is one of the most popular beach clubs on the island. The club offers a huge swimming pool, luxurious sun loungers, and a café providing wonderful cuisine and beverages.

Ark Bar Beach Club is renowned for its boisterous events, with DJs playing music till the early hours of the morning.

In conclusion, the beach clubs in Koh Samui, Thailand, provide a unique experience for guests. Whether you are searching for a lavish experience or a more laid-back ambiance, there is a beach club on the island that will meet your demands.

CHAPTER 6: DAY TRIPS FROM KOH SAMUI

Koh Samui, Thailand, is a picturesque island situated in the Gulf of Thailand. While there is enough to see and do on the island itself, there are also several day excursions that guests may take to explore the surrounding region.

From magnificent natural wonders to cultural activities, there is something for everyone on these day excursions.

One popular day excursion is to Ang Thong National Marine Park. This park is made up of 42 islands and is noted for its spectacular natural beauty. Visitors may take a boat tour of the park, go snorkeling or kayaking, and explore the various beaches and coves.

Another popular day excursion is to the neighboring island of Koh Phangan. This island is noted for its gorgeous beaches and active nightlife. Visitors may take a boat from Koh Samui to Koh Phangan and spend the day enjoying the island's various attractions.

For those interested in cultural activities, a day excursion to the adjacent town of Nathon is a must. This village is recognized for its traditional Thai architecture and local markets. Visitors may visit the town's various temples, enjoy local food, and buy gifts. Finally, for those searching for excitement, a day excursion to the surrounding forest is a terrific alternative. Visitors may go on a jungle hike, view waterfalls, and even go zip-lining through the treetops.

Overall, numerous day excursions from Koh Samui, Thailand provide a range of experiences for travelers. Whether you are interested in natural beauty, cultural experiences, or adventure, there is something for everyone on these day excursions.

Ang Thong National Marine Park

Ang Thong National Marine Park is a gorgeous natural beauty situated only a short boat ride away from Koh Samui, Thailand. This park is made up of 42 islands and is noted for its spectacular natural beauty, crystal-clear seas, and varied marine life.

A day excursion to Ang Thong National Marine Park is a must-do activity for anybody visiting Koh Samui, as it provides a unique and wonderful experience. The park is home to a diverse range of flora and animals, including tropical fish, sea turtles, and even dolphins.

Visitors may take a boat tour of the park, which enables them to see the various islands, beaches, and coves. The boat trip is a terrific opportunity to experience the park's various features, including the famed Emerald Lake, which is a gorgeous lagoon encircled by high cliffs.

One of the most popular activities at Ang Thong National Marine Park is snorkeling. The park's crystal-clear waters are home to a rich variety of marine life, including colorful fish, coral reefs, and even sea turtles. Visitors may rent snorkeling gear and explore the aquatic environment of the park.

Kayaking is another popular activity in the park. Visitors may hire kayaks and paddle across the park's various bays and lagoons. This is a terrific opportunity to discover the park's hidden beauties and get up close and personal with the park's natural splendor. For those searching for a more relaxed experience, the park's various beaches provide the ideal area to rest and soak up the sun.

Visitors may relax on the white sand beaches, swim in the crystal-clear seas, and enjoy the breathtaking views of the neighboring islands.

Overall, a day excursion to Ang Thong National Marine Park is a must-do experience for everyone visiting Koh Samui, Thailand. The park's spectacular natural beauty, rich marine life, and a broad choice of activities make it a unique and wonderful experience. Whether you are interested in snorkeling, kayaking, or just resting on the beach, there is something for everyone in this magnificent park.

Koh Tao Island

Koh Tao Island is a tiny but picturesque island situated off the coast of Koh Samui, Thailand. Known for its crystal-clear seas, vivid coral reefs, and abundant marine life, Koh Tao is a favorite destination for snorkeling and scuba diving lovers.

The island is also home to a variety of beaches, hiking trails, and other outdoor activities, making it a perfect location for tourists of all interests.

One of Koh Tao's biggest attractions is its world-class diving spots. The island is bordered by a variety of diving opportunities, ranging from small coral gardens to deep shipwrecks.

Divers may expect to observe a great variety of marine life, including colorful fish, sea turtles, and even whale sharks. Many dive shops on the island provide training and certificates for novices, as well as guided dives for more experienced divers.

For those who prefer to remain above water, Koh Tao also provides a range of snorkeling options. Visitors may rent snorkeling gear and explore the island's various coral reefs and small bays. Some of the better snorkeling spots on the island are Shark Bay, Mango Bay, and Tanote Bay.

In addition to its water sports, Koh Tao also provides a range of other outdoor activities. Visitors may climb to the island's several overlooks, including John-Suwan Viewpoint and Chumphon Viewpoint, for breathtaking panoramic views of the island and surrounding waters. The island is also home to several beaches, notably Sairee Beach, which is the longest and most popular beach on the island.

Koh Tao also boasts a thriving nightlife scene, with a range of clubs and restaurants catering to people from across the globe. The island's main town, Mae Haad, is home to a variety of stores, cafés, and restaurants, as well as a vibrant night market.

Overall, Koh Tao Island is a must-visit site for anybody visiting Koh Samui, Thailand. Its magnificent natural beauty, rich marine life, and a vast choice of activities make it a unique and memorable experience.

Whether you are interested in diving, snorkeling, hiking, or just resting on the beach, there is something for everyone on this lovely island.

Koh Phangan Island

Koh Phangan Island is a tropical paradise situated off the coast of Koh Samui, Thailand. Known for its magnificent beaches, active nightlife, and lush rainforest surroundings, Koh Phangan is a popular destination for vacationers from across the globe.

One of the biggest attractions of Koh Phangan is its world-famous Full Moon Party. This monthly event celebrated on the night of the full moon, brings thousands of party-goers to the island's Haad Rin Beach for a night of dancing, drinking, and partying.

The Full Moon Party is only one of several events conducted on the island throughout the year, including the Half Moon Festival and the Black Moon Culture Party.

But Koh Phangan is much more than simply a party destination. The island is home to several magnificent beaches, including Haad Yao, Thong Nai Pan, and Bottle Beach.

Visitors may sunbathe on the white sand beaches, swim in the crystal-clear seas, or try their hand at water sports like kayaking and paddle boarding.

For those who want to experience the island's natural beauty, Koh Phangan offers a range of hiking paths across its lush rainforest scenery. Visitors may climb the island's various waterfalls, including the famed Phaeng Waterfall, or visit the island's many temples and shrines.

Koh Phangan is also a renowned location for yoga and health retreats. The island is home to a variety of yoga studios and health facilities, providing anything from daily courses to week-long retreats. Visitors may also engage in spa treatments, meditation classes, and other wellness activities.

In addition to its natural beauty and therapeutic offers, Koh Phangan also boasts a bustling cuisine scene.

The island is home to a variety of restaurants and cafés, dishing customers everything from traditional Thai food to foreign specialties. Visitors may also try native street cuisine at the island's various night markets.

Overall, Koh Phangan Island is a must-visit site for anybody visiting Koh Samui, Thailand. Its magnificent natural beauty, active nightlife, and a vast choice of activities make it a unique and memorable experience.

Ang thong Discovery Tour

The Ang thong Discovery Tour is one of the most popular and highly recommended excursions for tourists visiting Koh Samui, Thailand.

This full-day cruise takes tourists on a voyage through the picturesque Ang thong National Marine Park, a group of 42 islands situated just off the coast of Koh Samui.

The trip starts with a pick-up from your accommodation in Koh Samui, and after a short drive, you will board the Aong National Marine.

On the boat journey itself, as you zoom through the crystal-clear waters of the passing breathtaking islands and rock formations along the route to Angth National Marine Park, you are welcomed by a scene of towering limestone cliffs, secluded lagoons, and pristine beaches.

The journey includes visits to some of the park's most picturesque islands, including Koh Mae Koh, Koh Wua Talap, and Koh Sam Sao.

At Koh Mae Koh, tourists may walk to the top of a steep stairway to reach the park's most renowned viewpoint, which offers panoramic views of the whole park. From there, tourists may take a short stroll to the park's Emerald Lake, a gorgeous lagoon surrounded by dense rainforest flora.

At Koh Wua Talap, tourists may relax on the beach, swim in crystal-clear waters, or explore the island's secret caverns and rock formations.

The island is also home to a small restaurant, where guests may have a delightful lunch of traditional Thai food.

At Koh Sam Sao, tourists may snorkel in the park's magnificent coral reefs, home to a variety of colorful fish and marine life. The island is also home to a magnificent beach, where tourists can relax and soak up the sun.

Throughout the trip, tourists will be escorted by an expert guide, who will give information on the park's history, ecology, and animals. The excursion also includes all essential equipment, including snorkeling gear and life jackets.

Overall, the Ang thong Discovery Tour is a must-do experience for everyone visiting Koh Samui, Thailand. The beautiful natural beauty of Ang thong National Marine Park, along with the excitement of a speedboat ride and the possibility to swim amid vivid coral reefs, makes this trip an amazing experience.

Samui Canopy Adventure

If you're seeking an exciting and unique way to explore the gorgeous woods of Koh Samui, Thailand, the Samui Canopy Adventure is the right day excursion for you. This eco-friendly adventure takes tourists on a zipline trip into the trees of the island's jungle, delivering spectacular vistas and an adrenaline-pumping experience.

The experience starts with a pick-up from your accommodation in Koh Samui and a short drive to the Samui Canopy Adventure base camp, nestled in the middle of the island's rainforest.

Upon arrival, tourists will be welcomed by pleasant and competent guides, who will offer a safety briefing and all essential equipment, including helmets, harnesses, and gloves. The zipline tour itself comprises 15 separate ziplines, ranging in length from 50 to 250 meters, and 21 various platforms, each presenting a unique view of the forest below. Visitors will fly over the trees, traversing over valleys and streams, and even whizzing past a magnificent waterfall.

In addition to the zipline tour, the Samui Canopy Adventure also contains a range of other activities, including a sky bridge, a spiral staircase, and a rappel fall. These activities provide a new sort of challenge and enable tourists to see the jungle from a fresh viewpoint.

Throughout the trip, tourists will be escorted by knowledgeable guides, who will present information about the jungle's flora and animals, as well as the history and culture of the island. The guides are also educated in first aid and rescue skills, assuring the safety of all tourists.

The Samui Canopy Adventure is appropriate for tourists of all ages and fitness levels, with no prior ziplining experience necessary. The trip is also eco-friendly, with an emphasis on maintaining the natural beauty of the forest and reducing the effect on the ecosystem.

Overall, the Samui Canopy Adventure is a must-do experience for everyone visiting Koh Samui, Thailand. The mix of adrenaline-pumping ziplining, magnificent vistas, and skilled operators make this trip an amazing encounter. Whether you're a nature lover, an adventure seeker, or just seeking a new way to explore the island, the Samui Canopy Adventure offers something for everyone.

CHAPTER 7:

ACCOMMODATION IN KOH

SAMUI

When it comes to housing, the island provides a broad selection of alternatives to suit every budget and inclination.

Luxury resorts and villas are available on Koh Samui, with many having private pools, beachfront access, and world-class facilities including spas, restaurants, and fitness centers. These villas are suitable for individuals wanting a high-end, luxurious holiday experience.

For those on a mid-range budget, there are lots of hotels and guesthouses to pick from, ranging from basic and economical to more premium and elegant.

Many of these homes include facilities such as swimming pools, restaurants, and beach access, making them a wonderful alternative for families and couples.

Budget tourists can also find lots of alternatives on Koh Samui, including hostels, guesthouses, and budget hotels. These homes provide modest facilities at a lower cost, making them suitable for travelers and people on a limited budget.

No matter what style of accommodation you pick, you can expect to discover pleasant and welcoming personnel, great Thai food, and breathtaking views of the island's natural beauty.

With so many alternatives to select from, Koh Samui is the ideal spot for a pleasant and relaxing trip.

Budget Hotels and Hostels

When it comes to housing, the island provides a broad selection of alternatives to suit every budget and inclination. For budget tourists, there are lots of alternatives on Koh Samui, including hostels, guesthouses, and budget hotels.

Hostels are a popular alternative for backpackers and budget tourists, providing economical lodging in a communal atmosphere.

Koh Samui offers various hostels distributed across the island, with costs ranging from as little as $5 per night to over $20 per night. These hostels provide basic facilities such as shared dorm rooms, communal restrooms, and common spaces for socializing. Some hostels also provide private rooms for people who desire more solitude.

One of the most popular hostels on Koh Samui is the Lub d Koh Samui Chaweng Beach hostel, situated in the middle of

Chaweng Beach. This hostel provides both dormitory and private rooms, with costs beginning at roughly $10 per night. The hostel also has a swimming pool, a rooftop bar, and a shared kitchen for guests to utilize.

Budget hotels are another choice for visitors searching for economical lodging on Koh Samui. These hotels provide basic facilities such as air conditioning, private toilets, and often a swimming pool. Prices for inexpensive hotels on Koh Samui vary from roughly $20 to $50 per night, depending on the location and facilities.

One famous budget hotel on Koh Samui is the Samui Heritage Resort, situated on Lamai

Beach. This hotel provides spacious rooms with air conditioning, private bathrooms, and a swimming pool, with pricing beginning at roughly $25 per night.

Guesthouses are also a popular alternative for budget vacationers on Koh Samui. These modest, family-run facilities provide basic lodging at a reasonable cost, with costs ranging from roughly $10 to $30 per night. Guesthouses generally offer a more personal touch, with pleasant employees and a warm ambiance.

One famous guesthouse on Koh Samui is the Samui Garden Home, situated near Bophut. This guesthouse provides pleasant rooms with air conditioning, private toilets, and a shared kitchen for guests to use. Prices start at roughly $15 per night.

Overall, budget visitors will find lots of alternatives for economical lodging on Koh Samui, including hostels, budget hotels, and guesthouses. While these alternatives may not provide the same degree of luxury as the island's high-end resorts and villas, they provide a comfortable and cheap base for exploring everything that Koh Samui has to offer.

Mid-Range Hotels and Resorts

The island is home to a broad assortment of hotels and resorts, catering to all kinds of guests. Among them, mid-range hotels and resorts are a popular alternative for travelers searching for a nice stay without breaking the budget.

Mid-range hotels and resorts in Koh Samui provide a choice of facilities and services that are excellent for tourists who wish to have a nice stay without spending too much money.

These hotels and resorts are often situated in great locations, near the beach and other popular attractions. They provide a choice of accommodation types, from ordinary rooms to suites, and are equipped with all the required facilities, like air conditioning, Wi-Fi, and flat-screen TVs.

One of the most popular mid-range hotels on Koh Samui is the Chaweng Regent Beach Resort. This resort is situated on the famed Chaweng Beach and provides a variety of facilities such as a swimming pool, spa, and fitness center.

The rooms are large and well-appointed, with contemporary facilities like air conditioning, Wi-Fi, and flat-screen TVs. The resort also boasts many eating choices, including a beachside restaurant and a poolside bar.

Another popular mid-range hotel on Koh Samui is the Samui Palm Beach Resort. This resort is situated on the calmer northern end of Chaweng Beach and provides a variety of facilities such as a swimming pool, spa, and fitness center. The rooms are large and well-appointed, with contemporary facilities like air conditioning, Wi-Fi, and flat-screen TVs. The resort also boasts many eating choices, including a beachside restaurant and a poolside bar.

For those searching for a more private and serene vacation, the Nora Buri Resort & Spa is a perfect alternative. This resort is built on a hillside facing the Gulf of Thailand and provides spectacular views of the water.

The rooms are large and well-appointed, with contemporary facilities like air conditioning, Wi-Fi, and flat-screen TVs.

The resort also boasts many eating choices, including a beachside restaurant and a poolside bar.

Overall, mid-range hotels and resorts on Koh Samui provide a perfect mix between comfort and price. They are great for those who wish to have a nice stay without spending too much money. With a selection of facilities and services, these hotels and resorts are a perfect option for anybody wishing to discover the beauty of Koh Samui.

Luxury Hotels and Villas

The island is also home to a broad choice of luxury hotels and villas, catering to guests who wish to indulge in the ultimate luxury experience. These hotels and villas provide a variety of facilities and services that are excellent for visitors searching for a luxury stay.

One of the most popular luxury hotels in Koh Samui is the Four Seasons Resort Koh Samui. This resort is built on a hillside facing the Gulf of Thailand and provides spectacular views of the water. The rooms and villas are large and well-appointed, with contemporary conveniences like air conditioning, Wi-Fi, and flat-screen TVs.

The resort also boasts many eating choices, including a beachside restaurant and a poolside bar.

The spa at the Four Seasons Resort Koh Samui is also a popular destination, providing a variety of treatments and services.

Another renowned luxury hotel on Koh Samui is the Banyan Tree Samui. This resort is built on a hillside facing the Gulf of Thailand and provides spectacular views of the water.

The villas are big and well-appointed, with contemporary conveniences such as air conditioning, Wi-Fi, and flat-screen TVs. The resort also boasts many eating choices, including a beachside restaurant and a poolside bar.

The spa at the Banyan Tree Samui is also a popular destination, providing a variety of treatments and services.

For those searching for a more quiet and private vacation, the Villa Mia is a perfect alternative. This magnificent property is set on a private beach and provides spectacular views of the ocean.

The villa is big and well-appointed, with contemporary conveniences such as air conditioning, Wi-Fi, and flat-screen TVs. The property also offers a private pool and many eating choices, including a beachside restaurant and a poolside bar.

The W Koh Samui is another famous luxury hotel on the island. This hotel is built on a hillside facing the Gulf of Thailand and provides spectacular views of the water. The rooms and villas are large and well-appointed, with contemporary conveniences like air conditioning, Wi-Fi, and flat-screen TVs.

The hotel also features many eating choices, including a beachside restaurant and a poolside bar. The spa at the W Koh Samui is also a popular destination, providing a variety of treatments and services.

Overall, luxury hotels and villas in Koh Samui provide the ultimate pleasure for guests who wish to enjoy the finest of what the island has to offer. With a selection of facilities and services, these hotels and villas are a perfect option for anybody wishing to indulge in the ultimate luxury experience.

Airbnb and Vacation Rentals

The island is also home to a broad selection of housing alternatives, including Airbnb and vacation rentals. These alternatives provide guests with a unique and original experience of the island, with a variety of facilities and services that appeal to diverse requirements and interests.

Airbnb and vacation rentals in Koh Samui provide a variety of alternatives, from budget-friendly flats to opulent villas. These alternatives are great for those who wish to experience the island like a local, with the freedom and flexibility to explore at their leisure. Many of these rentals are situated in ideal areas, with easy access to the beach, restaurants, and other attractions.

One of the most popular Airbnb and vacation rental alternatives in Koh Samui is the private villa. These villas provide a comfortable and isolated vacation, with facilities such as private pools, outdoor eating spaces, and breathtaking views of the ocean. Many of these villas also come with a personal chef and cleaning services, allowing for a sumptuous stay.

For those on a budget, there are also several economical Airbnb and vacation rental alternatives in Koh Samui. These alternatives include flats and guesthouses, which provide basic conveniences such as air conditioning, Wi-Fi, and cooking facilities.

These alternatives are great for those who wish to save money on lodging and spend more on touring the island.

Another popular Airbnb and vacation rental choice in Koh Samui is the beachfront villa. These bungalows give a unique and genuine experience of the island, with easy access to the beach and breathtaking views of the ocean.

Many of these bungalows also offer a variety of facilities, such as outdoor showers, hammocks, and private gardens.

Overall, Airbnb and vacation rentals in Koh Samui provide a unique and genuine experience of the island, with a choice of alternatives to meet various requirements and interests.

Whether you're searching for a magnificent villa or a budget-friendly apartment, there's something for everyone on Koh Samui. With magnificent beaches, crystal-clear oceans, and lush flora, Koh Samui is the ideal spot for a wonderful and unforgettable holiday.

CHAPTER 8: PRACTICAL INFORMATION

Welcome to Koh Samui, Thailand! This gorgeous island is noted for its breathtaking beaches, crystal-clear seas, and lush foliage. To help you make the most of your vacation, here is some practical advice and information:

1. Visa: Most tourists to Thailand may enter the country without a visa for up to 30 days. If you wish to remain longer, you will need to apply for a visa in advance.

2. Currency: The currency in Thailand is the Thai Baht (THB). ATMs are generally accessible on the island, and most establishments take credit cards.

3. Language: The official language of Thailand is Thai; however, English is commonly used in tourist regions.

4. Transportation: Taxis and tuk-tuks are accessible on the island, although they may be pricey. Renting a scooter or vehicle is a common alternative for getting about.

5. Weather: Koh Samui has a tropical environment, with temperatures varying from 25-35°C (77-95°F) throughout the year. The rainy season spans from September through November.

6. Lodging: Koh Samui provides a choice of lodging alternatives, from budget-friendly hostels to opulent villas. Airbnb and holiday rentals are other popular possibilities.

7. Activities: Koh Samui provides several activities, including snorkeling, diving, trekking, and visiting temples. The island is also renowned for its nightlife and shopping.

Currency and Exchange Rates

As a traveler, it is crucial to understand the currency and exchange rates of the nation to guarantee a smooth and hassle-free vacation. The currency of Thailand is the Thai Baht (THB), which is split into 100 satangs. The THB is widely accepted on the island, and

ATMs are accessible in most tourist locations. It is crucial to remember that certain ATMs may impose a fee for withdrawals; therefore, it is wise to verify with your bank before flying.

Exchange rates in Koh Samui might vary based on the area and the exchange provider. It is advisable to exchange money at authorized exchange booths or banks to prevent scams or counterfeit currencies.

The conversion rate for THB to USD is now approximately 30 THB to 1 USD, however, it is always advised to verify the current exchange rate before converting cash.

Credit cards are frequently accepted in Koh Samui, particularly in tourist areas and bigger enterprises. However, it is wise to bring cash for minor transactions or while going to more isolated sections of the island. When converting currencies, it is crucial to avoid losing money on exchange rates.

In addition, it is crucial to keep an eye on the currency rate while making purchases or reserving lodging. Some institutions may provide a better exchange rate than others, so it is recommended to browse around before making a purchase.

Overall, knowing the currency and conversion rates of Koh Samui, Thailand, is vital for every visitor. By being informed of the exchange rate and where to convert cash, tourists may assure a pleasant and hassle-free journey to this lovely island.

Language and Culture

Koh Samui, Thailand, is also home to a rich culture and language that are unique to the area. In this note, we will study the language and culture of Koh Samui, Thailand, in-depth.

Language: The official language of Thailand is Thai, and this is also the major language spoken on Koh Samui. However, given the island's reputation as a tourist destination, English is commonly spoken and understood in most tourist areas. In addition, many inhabitants on the island also speak Chinese, German, and French, among other languages.

The Thai language is a tonal language, which means that the meaning of a word may vary based on the tone used while saying it.

There are five tones in the Thai language, and it might take some time to learn them.

However, inhabitants on the island are typically tolerant and understanding when it comes to language obstacles, and they are always happy to assist tourists learn some basic Thai words.

Culture: The culture of Koh Samui, Thailand is profoundly based on Buddhism, and this is reflected in the island's numerous temples and shrines. The residents on the island are friendly and inviting, and they are always glad to share their culture with guests.

One of the major cultural events on the island is the Songkran Festival, which takes place in April. This celebration celebrates the Thai New Year, and it is celebrated with water battles, parades, and other activities.

Visitors to the island at this time should expect to get soaked in water by residents and other visitors alike, since this is a customary manner of enjoying the festival.

Another prominent cultural celebration on the island is Loy Krathong, which takes place in November.

This event is a celebration of the full moon, and it is characterized by the launching of miniature, decorated boats into the sea. These boats are fashioned from banana leaves and are adorned with flowers, candles, and incense. The releasing of these boats is supposed to signify the letting go of bad ideas and emotions.

In addition to these events, the culture of Koh Samui is also represented in its food, which is a combination of Thai and Chinese influences.

Visitors to the island may expect to enjoy a broad selection of delectable cuisine, including hot curries, fresh seafood, and sweets.

Overall, the language and culture of Koh Samui, Thailand, are an integral part of what makes this island such a unique and wonderful location.

By taking the time to learn some basic Thai words and by participating in local cultural activities, visitors visiting the island may develop a greater appreciation for the rich history and customs of this lovely area.

Koh Samui, Thailand, is a lovely island that draws millions of people every year. While the island is typically secure, it is vital to take basic steps to guarantee a safe and happy journey.

In this note, we will cover some safety considerations for tourists visiting Koh Samui, Thailand.

1. Be careful of your surroundings: As with any tourist attraction, it is crucial to be mindful of your surroundings at all times. Keep an eye out for any strange behavior and avoid wandering alone in remote locations, particularly at night.

2. Use common sense: Use common sense when it comes to your safety. Avoid carrying significant quantities of cash or valuables with you, and store your passport and other critical papers in a secure location.

3. Remain hydrated: Koh Samui may be hot and humid, so it is crucial to remain hydrated.

Drink lots of water and prevent excessive alcohol use, which may lead to dehydration and other health concerns.

4. Wear proper clothing: When visiting temples or other religious locations, it is necessary to dress correctly. This involves covering your shoulders and knees and avoiding exposing your apparel.

5. Choose respectable transportation: When utilizing transportation on the island, it is crucial to choose reliable firms. Avoid utilizing unregistered taxis or motorcycle taxis, since they may be risky and unreliable.

6. Be careful while swimming: While the beaches in Koh Samui are lovely, it is vital to be cautious when swimming. Always swim in approved locations and be mindful of any warning signs or flags.

7. Be careful while hiring motorcycles: Hiring a motorcycle may be a terrific way to explore the island, but it is necessary to be cautious. Always wear a helmet and drive conservatively, since the roads on the island may be small and twisty.

8. Be careful while using ATMs: While using ATMs on the island, be alert for any suspicious activities. Cover the keypad while typing your PIN, and avoid using ATMs in quiet places.

9. Be aware of scammers: Like every tourist location, Koh Samui has its fair share of fraud. Be careful of anybody offering you a bargain that appears too good to be true, and avoid providing money to strangers.

Overall, Koh Samui, Thailand, is a safe and fun place for travelers. By following these safety guidelines, travelers may assure a safe and pleasurable journey to this lovely island.

Useful Phrases

While English is commonly spoken on the island, it might be great to know some basic phrases in Thai to improve your experience and connect with people.

In this note, we will cover some of the most helpful terms to know while visiting Koh Samui, Thailand.

1. Sawadee krap/ka - Hello: This is a popular greeting in Thailand, with "krap" used by males and "ka" used by women.

2. Khob Khun krap/ka Thank you: This phrase is used to show thanks and admiration.

3. Mai pen rai: - No problem or You're welcome. This statement is intended to portray a feeling of easy-going ness and to reassure someone that there is no issue.

4. Sabai dee mai krap/ka - How are you?: This is a typical greeting that may be used to enquire how someone is feeling.

5. Sabai dee krap/ka I'm fine: This is a typical answer to the query, "Sabai dee mai krap/ka?"

6. Chai: - Yes: This is an easy method to say "yes" to a question.

7. Mai chai: - No: This is an easy way to say "no" to a question.

8. Ao: want: This is an important phrase to know when ordering food or beverages since it implies "want."

9. Mai ao: - Don't want. This is an important word to know when refusing anything since it signifies "don't want."

10. Nee tao rai krap/ka? How much is this? This is an important phrase to know while buying or bartering items.

11. Lot dai mai krap/ka? - Can you cut the price?: This is an important phrase to know while haggling for things.

12. Aroy - Delicious: This is an important word to know while enjoying food or beverages.

13. Mai aroy - Not delicious: This is a valuable word to know when expressing discontent with food or beverages.

14. Hong nam yoo tee nai krap/ka? - Where is the restroom?: This is a helpful phrase to know while hunting for a bathroom.

15. Khor thot krap/ka - Excuse me: This is a courteous approach to catch someone's attention or to apologize for anything.

Overall, understanding some basic Thai words might improve your experience while visiting Koh Samui, Thailand. By knowing these helpful words, you can speak with people, order food and beverages, and tour the island with ease.

Internet and Communication

One of the most vital features of any tourist location is connectivity, and Koh Samui boasts a well-developed internet and communication infrastructure that makes it simple for guests to remain connected.

Internet connectivity is generally accessible on Koh Samui, with most hotels, resorts, and restaurants providing free Wi-Fi to their customers. In addition, there are several internet cafés and mobile phone stores where guests may acquire SIM cards and data plans for their smartphones or tablets.

The island also boasts various internet service providers that provide high-speed internet connections to companies and households.

Communication on Koh Samui is very straightforward since English is commonly spoken on the island. Most residents working in the tourist business, such as hotel employees, restaurant waiters, and tour guides, speak English proficiently. In addition, many signs and menus are printed in both Thai and English, making it easier for tourists to explore the island.

For individuals who wish to acquire some basic Thai words, there are several language institutions and private tutors on Koh Samui that provide Thai language sessions. Learning some basic Thai words will enrich your stay on the island and help you converse with locals.

In terms of mobile phone coverage, Koh Samui enjoys great service from all major mobile phone companies.

Visitors may acquire SIM cards at the airport or mobile phone outlets on the island. International roaming is also possible, although it might be pricey, thus, it is advisable to obtain a local SIM card and data package.

For people who need to make international calls, there are several internet cafés and phone businesses that provide international calling services at cheap prices. In addition, several hotels and resorts provide international calling services for their visitors.

Overall, Koh Samui boasts a well-developed internet and communication infrastructure that makes it simple for guests to remain connected. With free Wi-Fi, mobile phone service, and language schools, travelers can easily interact with locals and keep connected with friends and family back home.

CONCLUSION

Koh Samui, Thailand, is a magnificent island that provides a unique combination of natural beauty, cultural legacy, and contemporary facilities. From beautiful beaches and lush rainforests to ancient temples and lively marketplaces, Koh Samui offers something for everyone. Whether you are a solitary traveler, a couple on a romantic trip, or a family on a fun-filled holiday, Koh Samui has lots to offer.

One of the most vital features of any holiday location is connectivity, and Koh Samui boasts a well-developed internet and communication infrastructure that makes it simple for guests to remain connected. With free Wi-Fi, mobile phone service, and language schools, travelers can easily interact with locals and keep connected with friends and family back home.

In addition to communication, Koh Samui provides a broad choice of activities and attractions. Visitors may discover the island's natural beauty by trekking through the woods, swimming in the crystal-clear seas, or resting on the beach.

For those interested in culture and history, there are numerous old temples and historical monuments to visit, including the Big Buddha Temple and the Fisherman's Village.

Koh Samui is also renowned for its active nightlife, with numerous pubs, clubs, and restaurants providing live music, dancing, and entertainment. Visitors may spend a night out on the town, trying local food and beverages, or just relaxing and enjoying the environment.

Overall, Koh Samui is a must-visit place for everyone visiting Thailand. With its natural beauty, historic legacy, and contemporary comforts, it provides a unique and remarkable experience.

Whether you are seeking adventure, leisure, or a little bit of both, Koh Samui offers something for everyone. So, pack your luggage, buy your tickets, and get ready for a memorable adventure to Koh Samui, Thailand.

Recommendations for First-Time Visitors

For first-time tourists, it might be hard to determine what to do and where to go. Here are some tips to help make your vacation to Koh Samui unforgettable:

1. Explore the Island's Natural Beauty: Koh Samui is famed for its magnificent beaches, thick forests, and crystal-clear seas. Take a day excursion to Ang Thong National Marine Park, where you can enjoy snorkeling, kayaking, and hiking.

Visit the Hin Ta and Hin Yai Rocks, which are natural rock formations that mimic male and female genitalia. Take a swim in the Na Muang Waterfall, which is one of the island's most famous attractions.

2. Experience the Local Culture: Koh Samui has a rich cultural legacy, and there are numerous temples and historical places to visit. Visit the Big Buddha Temple, which is one of the island's most recognizable sights.

Take a walk around Fisherman's Village, which is a lovely region full of traditional Thai residences, stores, and restaurants. Attend a Thai cooking class, where you can learn how to create classic meals like Pad Thai and Tom Yum Soup.

3. Enjoy the Nightlife: Koh Samui boasts a busy nightlife, with numerous pubs, clubs, and restaurants providing live music, dancing, and entertainment. Visit the Chaweng Beach district, which is noted for its bustling atmosphere and party scene. Check out the Ark Pub, which is a renowned seaside pub that holds nightly parties and events.

4. Try the Local food: Thai food is recognized for its intense flavors and fresh ingredients. Sample local cuisine, including Pad Thai, Tom Yum Soup, and Green Curry.

Visit the night markets, where you may enjoy street cuisines such as grilled meats, fish, and fried snacks. Take a culinary class, where you may learn how to create traditional Thai cuisine.

5. Rest and Unwind: Koh Samui is also a terrific spot to rest and unwind. Book a spa treatment where you can luxuriate in a Thai massage or aromatherapy session.

Take a yoga session where you can practice mindfulness and meditation. Lounge on the beach, where you can soak up the sun and enjoy the coastal air. Koh Samui is a must-visit place for everyone visiting Thailand. With its natural beauty, historic legacy, and contemporary comforts, it provides a unique and remarkable experience.

By following this advice, you may make the most of your vacation to Koh Samui and create experiences that will last a lifetime.

SCAN THE QR CODE BELOW TO GET ACCESS TO MORE BOOKS BY ME

Made in the USA
Monee, IL
31 January 2024

52715516R00098